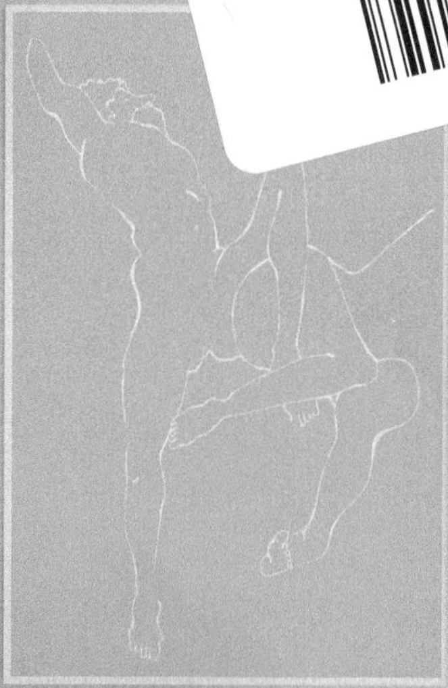

Within-land

Journeying Through
Grief, Confusion, Heartbreak & Hope

DANAE K. FROESE

Illustrations By Callen Froese

FriesenPress

One Printers Way
Altona, MB R0G0B0,
Canada

www.friesenpress.com

First Edition — 2021

ISBN
978-1-03-910829-5 (Hardcover)
978-1-03-910828-8 (Paperback)
978-1-03-910830-1 (eBook)

Poetry, Subjects & Themes, Death, Grief, Loss

Distributed to the trade by The Ingram Book Company

Table of Contents

"To navigate because you see more of the context"

—Michelle

Mourners

Fear-land

Sorrow and Heartbreak

Too Soon I Am Old

What do I have to say?
My heart is empty,
My lips are numb.
Inside my mind run circles.
The day comes and goes
In a passing breath.
Once I was young,
Too soon I am old.

Thoughts From Within a Taupe Bedroom

The morning light illuminates the terracotta pots on my sill.
The greenery lives but does not thrive.
It is in tune with my heart—
The way I nurture, the way I neglect.
The ceramic cat from my childhood is left with a
chipped ear.
He sat on the shelf of my last relationship.
He came through after the last broken heart.
We are on our own now.
The taupe-coloured room leaves little to the imagination.
My things are now gathered in this space,
Reminding me of dreams yet to be conceived,
Of adventures yet to be lived,
Of lovers yet to be adored,
A son deceased never to be mothered—
Me, woman, motherhood denied.
Is that how you see me?
Damn you.
Unfit.
The Spiderwort thrives in partial shade—
Its silvery green reflects light hidden among shadow.
Where has my heart gone?
I have lost her again—
She is always off wandering.
She will be back.

This Wicked World

She wants to chew me up and spit me out.
Today, she is winning.
I weep rivers and sink valleys with my begging knees.
She laughs in spite of me.
I go on without pay.
Take pity,
I beg.
"Take heart,"
She coos.
All malice, wiped from her lips, as she's had her fill.
She sees me and I tremble.

Dirty Dishes

I had left for only a short while.
The ceilings—
They were too high.
The cats followed me around—
One of them, anyways.
The other lay unmoving for hours—
Was he dead?
I did the dishes my way—
Wrong,
But I didn't care.
I turned the heat up high on the stove—
. . . I did oil the cutting board—
Right.
It was cracking.
He had made it, and was very proud.
It was well made.
Not to my taste—
Anyways.
There were rules.
I would break them and be in trouble.
I felt like a quivering child—
Forgiven by their parent only after a good talking to.
I was indignant,
Not sorry.
I was caught again.
I tried food that came from a box.
God, it was terrible! We really shouldn't eat that—
No one should eat that.

It is just a difficult time—
Pandemic—
You know.
Oh, but the love I had felt, so keen and bright,
Was snuffed out.
It left as quickly as the flame ignited.
His eyes assessed me.
I am a good cook.
Leave me alone—
I know how to use cast iron pans.
Leave me alone.
My boss had trusted me all those years ago, and I didn't know anything—
Or maybe I did.
He saw that—
Why can't you?
Don't you trust anyone?
There was no sex—
Not really, anyways.
Once a week, at best—
I counted.
We are young and beautiful!
But it wasn't practical.
It came at a cost—
Didn't I understand?
But he loved me—
Did he?

Friend of Sorrow

I now know sorrow—
Like a good friend.
I understand our relationship—
And its purpose.
I understand the deep love—
The granite truths.
I let sorrow comfort me,
Wrap its arms about me,
Hold me, and rock me to sleep.
Every teardrop is letting go,
Every howl,
Every agonizing sob.
And then sorrow comes to me.
I am never alone
Sorrow is with me, holding my hand.

Oh, Death

Oh, death.
Oh, death.
You brought me the light;
I hate to see such a sight.

Oh, death.
Oh, death.
You brought me the light;
Have mercy, have mercy
On me.

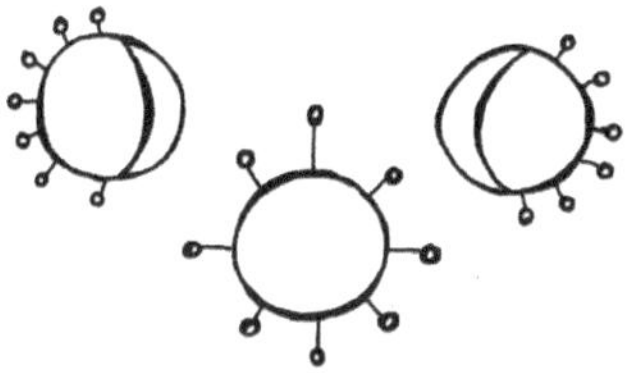

Natural Disaster

The end was crippled,
Splintered at the knee.
Bitter flames licked at the edges of meagre remnants,
Consuming what was left.
A natural disaster, some claim;
But we are not fooled—
We know who brought on the landslide;
We know who lured the rising tide;
We know who swept the winds
Into a raging storm,
Ripping trees out from their rooted homes,
Casting corpses idly aside,
As if to say,
You deserve this;
Pain begets pain.
Quitter, you roared from your towering height.
Acid rain, you poured;
And bitter tears, I wept.

Your level of understanding and commitment to loving me
Is a disgrace.
Quitter,
Quitter,
Quitter,
Quitter,
QUITTER.
Poetry, isn't it;
I didn't write it, but I will take the credit.
His broken words
Cut like glass—
Leaving blood dripping from my ears.
I am sorry I shorthanded your creativity.
But it was too late for sorry.
Rain wept down my cheeks.

Pisces

What are my eyes but the fish of my soul
Swimming in salted oceans.

Spinning

What is it —
That time and time again
I forget . . . ?

What was that?
Where was I going?
Where did I come from?
What do I like?
Who am I?
Where did I go?

My skin cries out in anger as my stomach bloats,
As my last breath catches in my chest.
My brow knits tight and knots—
Bang! Bang! Bang!
She has had another seizure!
No, it is the neighbour's children upstairs.
Ten-thirty now. Do they ever retire?
Do I?
False alarms keep me on my toes.
Again, I grapple for breath.
One dead son;
One abusive boyfriend;
And three broken hearts later . . .
. . . I can't breathe and wonder why.
No money.
One pandemic.
Food shortages, worldwide, and I drink oat milk—
Well, of course, cow's milk gives me dandruff and

terrible digestion—
What was that?
Digestion . . .
Where was I going?
Who am I?

Her Heart Weeps

Her *heart*
Weeps,
And weeps,
And weeps.
Her eyes—
Waterbeds
Of flowers.
The soil dense with sorrowful drops;
Their heads bow in grief
            They are *so* respectful.
"Thank you, dearly," she whispers with one hand on her heart.
"You are so kind—
"So kind."

Questioners

Plea-land

Defeat and Confusion

A Job Posting

Nothing.
Still.
No fire; no sparks.
Where is the light?
Maybe gasoline.
A lack of kindling...
Yes! Kindling
What would it be?
Where do I find it?
I went out listening but heard nothing.
Where were the angels this time?
Was it because I shut down?
Stopped listening?
Criticized their work?
Have they quit me, the way I have quit everything and everyone else?
The way that I quit myself.
What if I put out a job posting?
No.
That wouldn't do.
They might like it if I began to sing.
I am out of the ability.
Why is that—
It quit me too?
Is this a poem—
Or just words without proper punctuation?

Colours and Bright Lights

And again—
The day escapes me.
Like a prisoner cloaked in a veil of night,
I am deceived at every turn,
Distracted by all of the colours and bright lights.
No wiser than a young child—
New to this withering world.

Broken Pieces of Wishful Thinking

For 26 years, she built on a broken foundation.
She can go no further;
She can bear no more weight.
Dreams slip like landslides.
She suffocates, buried by debris.
There is but a heap—
Broken pieces of wishful thinking.
They cut like glass.
Jagged edges bleed heels as she treads—
Inoculating disease.
She festers.

Change

The gardens have been paved—
Made room for children's play.
Could they not play in the dirt?
Wonder at the secret world of the plant—
Of the insect,
Of the worm,
Of the soil—
The lonely apple tree
Cut back.
I know what they have done to the insides—
Linoleum, I heard.
The cast-iron tub and sink thrown away.
That house is over one hundred years old, you know.
The hardwood floors carried rumour of past lives.
On occasion, I would hear them whisper,
As I shuffled across the dining-room floors.
The elms are dying—
Disease.
We wanted them for their beauty, and sentenced them to
lives in detrimental mono-population.
The park has long since been demolished.
Plastic.
Disease.
They cut down the climbing tree at Gregory's house—
It didn't fit the esthetic.

I Want to Be There

So what do I do?
So much beckons and calls—
And I want to abandon them all.
I wake with a start,
With questioning in my heart,
With my mind racing and flogging me:
"Get up, go!
"You have much to do.
"You never complete a task,
"Or follow through."
My shoulders rise to my ears—
I want to be small;
I want to disappear.
I cannot seem to light the life-giving fire.
I remember the days when I was young—
Spending long hours beneath
A summer's relentless sun;
Without thought beyond pulling weeds.
I want to be there,
With the warmth spreading throughout my mop of dark hair,
Where I do not question my heart,
Where I am whole, not falling apart.
I want to be there.

Disgruntled

What are you doing with your day?
Doesn't really matter, anyways.
As long as I'm not extracting oil,
Building pipelines,
Or turning the soil;
As long as I'm not part of war, I'm all right.
What about a career?
Don't make me laugh so, my dear
I've got a stitch in my side.
I can't breathe.
You're way out of line.
As long as I'm not part of war, I'm all right.
What are you going to do with your life—
Aside from what I do today?
I wake up and find a way
Of making it through the laughable day,
To keep from turning myself in.
As long as I'm not part of war, I'm all right—
        I'm doing all right.

But do I really have a say?
We are all conscripted, anyway.
From the day that I was born,
I was housed in concrete.
Plastic.
Oh, lord.
Packaged food and Internet;
Taking pets to the vet;
Turning on and tuning out—
You can't really count you out.
Waging war against the earth
Through passive means like giving birth
As long as I'm not part of war I'm all right—

I'm doing all right.

It Was Me

Frustration floods my heart.
I cannot see beyond the
I—
What do *I* want?
What do *I* need?
Where am *I* going?
Who am *I*?
What is *my*—
My— my— my— my— *MY*—
It is time to abandon the *me*.
Time to forget
There is so much more.
Goodbye, it wasn't you; it was me.

Looking Down

Where does the light go when it fades—
The soul when the body dies—
The sound once it's filled its time?
How do we mend a heart when it breaks?
How do we find joy in an ache?
Where is life at the bottom of a pit?
How do we find it—
When life is to be lived,
But you find yourself with nothing left to give?
Do you go on?
What is being when the heart is blue?
How is loving when the heart is without lungs—
Without oxygen—
Without breath?
What is breath without the heart?
Can we ache without a heart?
Is ache in the breaking—
In the mending—
In the undoing?
Where did we leave joy when we left it behind?
Is it swept beneath a rug
Or along with time?
What is sorrow?
How does it drape?
How does it manage to suffocate and snuff?
How do we light the candle once it is spent?
Where do we find wax,
Wick,

Friction,
Heat,
Flame,
Fire?
How do we find our way back from lost?
How do we pull ourselves from stuck?
Where did we leave play?
I could have sworn I saw her just the other day.
Why is it we continue to fall?
Is it because we looked down?

Peace, Peace, Peace

The memory is mere particles now—
Dust and water and air.
Her eyes no longer see clearly;
She is almost certain of her past.
Yes, she was a warrior—
A fighter—
A brave girl.
She has grown old in her youth;
She has grown crippled in her fear.
Like a lifetime spent in cold bath water,
Hypothermia has set in.
The chill rattles her bones;
She is nothing but the cold.
But that is not quite right.
Life, however small, is life, nonetheless.
The roots, however withered and dried, remain in soil.
She pines for sunlight.
Sunlight, she groans,
Like those lost in the deserts heat.
"God, I beg of you—
"This is my dark hour;
"Will you not come to me?"

"But you did not love me when the tide was high—
"When the air was cool,
"Or when fresh dew hung like diamonds off a leaf."

"I was blind; I was mistaken; I was afraid.
"But what of now?

"If you see,
"If you now know,
"If you are fearless,
"Why then do you call upon me?"
"I see that I cannot go any longer on my own.
"I know that without your love, I am lost.
"I quiver like a calf on its virgin limbs.
"Fear—
"I am afraid of you,
"Of life,
"Of death,
"Of eternity,
"Of an end,
"And of everything that lies in between."

I pray you lighten my heart.
I yearn for lightness.
I yearn for brightness—
Weightlessness,
Clarity,
Simplicity—
Peace,
Peace,
Peace.
I yearn.
My heart.

"If you yearn for lightness, put down your load.
"If you yearn for brightness, turn on the light.
"If you are yearning for weightlessness,
"Go find yourself in a body of water.

"If you yearn for clarity, clean the lens
"If you want for simplicity, do not complicate.
"And peace,
"Peace,
"Peace—
"It is yours when you accept it.
"Like a long lost lover who awaits your return,
"Invite them in.
"It is cold outside and it will be winter soon,"`

Alive and the Living

What does it take to reawaken the spirit—
To breathe life back into the lungs,
To instil joy,
Laughter,
Peace,
A deeper sense of belonging,
Acceptance beyond words,
Knowing beyond understanding,
There is alive,
Then there is living?
What ignites the spark?
What catches the flame?
What burns low and hot?
What is it that sustains?
Where is the wood we gather to dry,
Within our forests deep?
How do we keep our forests alive,
While finding space to rest?

ADD

What would it be like to—
I don't know; I'm not really.
It is quite lovely, isn't—
The grass was green yesterday but—
How did we get—
I'd like to go back to—
Hey, hold on a—
Do you remember when—
Can you fix the—
Remind me, where was—
Tomorrow we will find—
Would you—
Oh you, good—
Okay then, when—
I can't seem to get—
A little bit sweeter, it's—
Sigh . . .

The Bread Baker from Upstairs

There's banging coming from upstairs again.
Sam went to ask,
"Um, would you mind?"
The door opens, but ajar,
Producing a sliver of a women's face.
"I'm so sorry; I'm making bread."
Bread.
Hmm.
I've made bread.
Strange.
What am I doing wrong?
What am I missing?
Does bread hurt?
Does bread slap?
Does bread weep?
What do you do when the neighbours from upstairs are baking bread?

Ramblings of a Drifter

The virus has killed so many—
I'm wondering if I'll be one to go.
I'm walking past a synagogue now with doors closed—
Not even a God's hope.

Traffic, distant as a bird's song.
Do I condemn this pandemic,
When the silence I crave has fallen?
My loved ones still stand;
I am the lucky one,
Making hast to the countryside with a lover.
Again, my life is packed away in plastic boxes—
A backpacker's dream.
My home?
My room?
No more;
Not again.
How can I love space in the same way I love him?
How is it I feel freedom within my rigid taupe box?
Is it the warm brown of the veneer—
The solid wood dresser,
With curved, carved grooves bowing in at the forehead like lovers.
Is it the rooting plants on my window sill—
New growth green from the waters mildew?
What more do I need?
The poetic ripple of piano conducts
As I tap tap tap.
The colourful array of melody embraces my heart and spins

it round within its capturing arms;
There I dance and sway.
The sunlight filters in;
She is my guest.
What more do I need?
Do not force me out,
Please.
I am safe here;
No wounds to make here;
I am whole; I am somebody here.
Picasso prints clipped to a board decorate my mind.
Cheap, I know.
They bring me joy, nonetheless.
Out there, they want more of me;
In here, I am enough.
Please—
I will be good;
I will be content.
A haunting melody suggests I turn the knob of my door;
My curiosity is piqued.
How dare the song betray me—
Leading me astray from my own sanctuary.
The stores were empty;
They were closed.
Why does that make me happy?
The peace that I yearn is settling the life that I call to
is beckoning—
I am packed.

Life's Broken Promise

My heart pounds at her ribbed cage—
Ka thunk, ka thunk, ka thunk.
My mind soothes—
"Love, you cannot make it on your own."
I am a starved heroin—
Crawling,
Hands and knees across barren wastelands—
Teetering between life's broken promise and
death's guarantee.
Each day too short for work;
Each day too short for play;
Each day too short for rest;
Each day too short to hunger;
Each day too short to thirst.
Each day too short.

All Rise

Listless, where is life?
Where is the spark to ignite
A flame?
I am so flat—
Drawn out thin and worn.
I am in the midst of my youth!
Why do I weep so heavily as though all has been turned against me?
Where are my bright eyes,
My intrigue, and curiosity?
Where is the fire as the morning light bursts from the shadows?
Where is the urge to run,
To fly, to soar?
There is a sky—an endless horizon.
How can I be so tired?
My beauty will run its course;
My muscles and bones exhaust.
So today, rise!
All rise.
What is it that excites—
That pulls me from my shell?
God, I am worn;
Woe, I am worn.
Today,
I say,
Today, I will find a way.
For how many days now have I uttered these words?

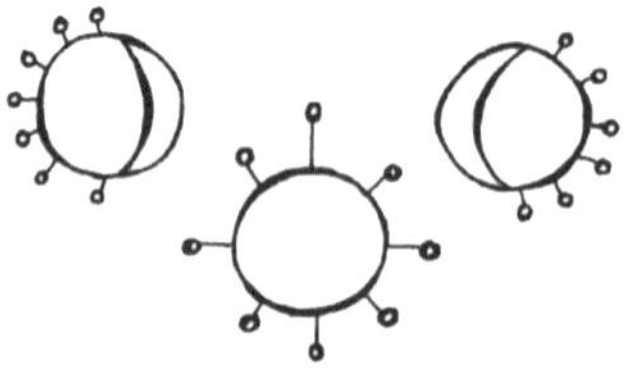

The Seasons of Amour

What do we do when words fall shy—
When the cupboards are emptied,
When store shelves wait barren,
When the skies unfailing hues mute to a deadpan grey,
When the seasons meet and collide—
And it is never summer,
Never winter,
Never fall,
And never spring?

What do we do when tender souls embrace,
But the laces are rugged and worn—
When skipping stones sink,
When the moon ceases to shed light,
When hearts break and cannot mend?
They hold out,
Weep and defend,
Build walls,
And barricade?

Am I Zero

Am I guilty?
Crap television and too much food.
Am I worthy,
Wise?
Are they like a positive and negative sign—
One cancelling out the other of equal value?
Am I zero?
Is this poetry,
Or is it crap—
Is it just zero?

Uncertainty

This time, my love, I am not so sure—
Did I walk away like a fool—
Without certainty,
Without clarity?
My eyes do not weep, but my heart has left me;
She is out wondering the streets late into the night.
Where she wanders, I dare not ask.
What will she want from me?
What will she ask of you?

My mind is a fog without my heart;
My chest knots and coils.
I have long since parted with my babe deceased—
Though his picture is here right now,
Next to me as I wonder,
As I fumble through days as delicate as a flower's petal.
I have bid my farewells and shed a fair tear.
My hands beg to be soiled;
My brow furls for sweat;
My belly yearns to feel hunger so as to feel satiated
once more.

For you, I am numb;
For you, I am cold;
For you, I am stiff and refusing.
I feel nothing but the pit of my belly and shortness
of breath.
What is it about love that tortures me?
For you, I was sure;

For you, I was brave.
But we crumbled under pressure,
And I feared the lack of lovemaking,
Dancing, and play;
I feared the dinners without pleasure and gratitude—
I will not go on.

I have not been sure in some time.

Heartbreakers

Dream-land

Body and Sex

Tall Grass Prairies

Caress me, darling.
Fondle my moistened cunt.
She's wetted for her lover,
In the dream.
Her legs are splayed open.
Nakedness lies beneath her light summer dress.
A hand lingers over her purring *minou*.
He is no more than a known stranger,
Welcome to her foreign lands.
Revelry—
Paralyzed in pleasure, he presses onwards,
Inwards.
Her breath catches in a
Huu
          Huu
                    Huu
          Huuuu

He is down on his knees,
Mouth-kissing her ocean of desire.
Her waves lap his cheeks,
Chin—
Running down his neck.
Together, they sway in rhythm
Of the tall prairie grasses.

There Is a Love that Lingers

A love that flickers,
In and out of existence—
A fire that ignites of its own accord,
Own breath—
Wind;
Friction;
From the remaining coals,
At the bottom of the pit fire;
The gentle breath of seasons changed,
Gathers kindling to the smouldering flame;
Sparkling laughter dazzles in the back of a mind
As the brown leaf ignites!
But nay—
Nay—
Nay—
There is a pain that lingers,
A hurt that aches,
Agitated by a brief thought—
A catalogued memory—
Extinguishing all that was,
Is,
Could have been

Good;
Dampened by generations—
Of fear,
Greed,
Ego—
There was love.
Where was love?
Was love there?
There is a love that lingers.

Passion the Fruit

Moisture—a film between skins.
Hallowed moans escape
As hunting fingers penetrate;
Warmth emanates,
Rising like steam from a warm bath;
Encased in tile and frigid air,
Tongues savour the sweet,
Suckle the sour,
Indulge in the savoury
And the scent.
          Uggghhh
                    Siiigh
Hmmmm
Deep inhales—
Corners of the body dubbed ill
By a misunderstanding
Now savoured,
          Devoured
          Indulged
Radiant in heat—

An odour so potent, so pure, escapes.
Consumed in gasps,
Tones of spice, of earth and breath,
Bring new life,
Arise in the air in full blossom.
Hold me, my sweet.
          Escaped whispers
Closer to me.
          Parted lips beg
Naked skin seeped in moisture,
Like that of ripe fruit,
From the passion just had.
Limbs encircle bodies.
Bodies—front to front—tenderly
Embrace.
This is love.
          This is love
                    This is love
This is love

Lover of My Imaginings

I crave to be held by lover's arms—
For the breath caught in my throat to be released.
Could his enduring embrace release me?
In my dream, he was angry and wild.
His hunger was anger, and he flogged me.
Is this lover of my imagining just that—
A fallacy;
A honeyed dream;
A sweet taste of churned ice cream;
A spot of dew on the morning's crisp mint;
A shape in the clouds bound to shift;
A story spun through a romantic's haze;
A glimpse of moonbeam during the light of day?
I crave the kiss of a lover's warm mouth—
For the pit of sorrow within me to be filled.
Could his tongue and lip lift me from these depths?
The last time our lips brushed swift,
I silently begged for a lasting embrace—
One that would lead to lovemaking—
He told me that it came at a price.

This lover must be of my imaginings—
A wild tale;
A bowl of summer strawberries and cream;
A memory of a past life;
A promise made with fingers tied;
A cotton candy on a stick;
A whisper passed through prairie grasses tall;
A warmth enduring through the winter's season.

Rainy Day Fund

Do you believe in me?
I can tell by that glint in your eye.
I can see.
Do you deceive me?
Wait until a slip or troubled sleep;
By night, you dare creep,
And find me in a vulnerable state,
Thieving all belief,
All that was there, all that was cultivated with care—
You take it back;
You put it away—
Save it all for a rainy day.
And when I threaten to go,
Belief in my heart,
Seeds you sow,
Plant them there—
I'll water them with my own tears.
But this you already know, my dear.
This is your trick—
Your wicked way.

Honey

Honey,
This morning I remembered
Orange, Mediterranean Sky blue, mustard yellow, fiery red,
dusty pink, dusty blue—
I love these colours.
Did you know that?
I had forgotten.
What else?
Flowers—
But you knew that one, didn't you?
I am still afraid—
Stifled,
Nervous.
Don't wait, honey—
Grow.
Go find yourself a home—
A comfort.
Curl up—
Take comfort.
Find a place of ease for your unsteady heart to beat.

Another Lover

Another lover
Languished
And lost
To the tide of lovers past,
To join in the chorus,
Cries . . .
"We *loved* you"
You were "*Exceptional*"
"My love"
"There was something *special*"
Passions soured,
Like spilt milk left unattended.
She was . . .
"*Loathsome*"
"Broken" "A project"
"A *secret*"
"Difficult"
. . . but never boring.

A love affair—
Fragmented;
An empty project sought in haste.
I tried to listen to my heart—
She had fallen silent.
She was still

Did she feel love?
Did she feel pain?

To him I plead,
"I miss you; I love you."
Love me, please.
Love me with your words.
Fill the hollow which you have so delicately carved
within me.
But it's not practical, not productive.
No, we wouldn't want to waste our time.
Please, let us make love.

Did I leave you because of the sex?—
Because you would not enter me,
Lick me,
Grab me,
Graze me,
Taste me,
Suckle me,
Observe me,
Long for me,
Press your heightened state against me,
Expose yourself to me?—
Because I could not bite you,
Excite you,
Suck you,
Ride on top of you,
Slowly enter you,
Thirst for you,
Whisper in your excitable ear,
Oh, my dear, yes!?
I seek passion—
A lover's dream—

Heated desire, my love.
My honey, please don't weep.
        God, I want to hold your head in my lap.
But it is at my word
        That you tremble—
At my parting, you fall to your knees.
Why wouldn't you make love to me?

Bad Breasts

Stretched—
Etched—
Deflated—
Deformed—
My breasts are no longer socially acceptable.

Our Love

Oh my dear,
My heart thumps inside my chest,
Like a wild rabbit trapped by its predator,
Caught in a frenzy of panic, fear, and uncertainty.
Our love was like the snow—
Effortlessly tumbling from the heavens
As nature intended,
As the turn of the season beckoned.
Our love was like the flower—
Innocent in its youth,
Full in its blossom.
Our love was like the breeze—
Gentle in its nature,
Precious with its sweet whisper.
But fear, my dear—
The worry, the past.
I have been a bird before—
Caged.
I have forgotten flight—
What it is to spread my wings and soar yonder.
I am sorry, my dear, but you do hinder me—
Crowd my ceaseless mind—
Barricade the clear path—
Curtail the endless musings of my mind.
It is not within your aim to take the wind
From my chest,
To leave me gasping,
Short of breath.

Love in the Back Forty

Nakedness and touch—
Love in the back forty—
Fondling in the woods.
Sweets dripping from the lips of the ravenous;
Music from the lips of the good people;
Murmurs from the lips of the satiated lovers.
The festivities are alight—
The grounds consumed by dancers,
By joy makers,
By trouble seekers,
By prank players,
By lovers,
By playmates,
By magic enchanters,
By hoop dancers,
By food eaters,
. . . sigh
Isn't it wonderful!
A large fire ablaze, as night begins to fall.
Children lay dreaming in corners,
Strewn across the hay;
It is time for the grownups to play,
And play and play all night—
Until, by the early mornings light, do they render
themselves weary.

Lover and Her Fool

Come and caress me, my dear;
I long desperately for your touch—
My dreams laced with the heat of other men.
Do not fear; I yearn for you—
But my mind, my body—
I dream up lavish tails of entanglement,
Of my name whispered sweetly,
Of my insides penetrated, slowly and deeply.
I long for throes of passion,
For desperate hunger in each other's mouths—
Spread wide—
Tongues wetting the dried corners of my wilted lips,
Hands grabbing at the supple skin of my cushioned torso,
Words exchanged in low pleading tones,
Of lust.
Ask me what I like,
Pull me to you,
Push me down.
My fighting isn't for release—
No—
But for more.
The sounds that escape our parted lips make me sweat
Sweet droplets of heated desire.
You capture these on your tongue and are quenched.
Oh god, oh god, oh god, oh god—
God knows
All of our secrets.
I am mischievous—

My heart and my groin are at play;
Come play with me, you fool.

Good Lover

Good lover at the nape of my neck,
On your knees on the floor,
Begging *please*—
I will give you more.

A Passionate Summer's Eve

How I weep at the very thought of you—
In joy and in pain
In delight and in sorrow
In staying and in the nagging desire to go.
I am wrought with confusion—
Ensconced by fear.

And the flowers—rich, dense hues of purple, violet, and clean opaque white—
Bore as a gift from your tender heart,
Inhale stale air,
Breathing unto me, purity,
Yet I choke.

I am stifled and broken down
By the sharp edges of your pointed tongue.
I beg of thee,
Speak unto me only the words that soften,
As butter does upon a wooden table
On a passionate summer's eve.

Faith Holders

Hope-land

Healing and Renewal

Be Still!

Clever exhaustion—
You rob me of my chores,
Desires,
Expectations,
Goals—

Nay—

Relieve me—
Demanding I stop to rest;
Demanding I stop to see;
Demanding that I stop to listen;
Demanding I be still—
Be still! You command.
I am withered—
Too tired,
Too drawn out,
Too thin
To refuse.
At first, I rest and inflict self-hatred—
You lazy, unmotivated, unaccomplished failure.
At first, when I look about, I snarl in disgust—
I see what is broken, what is wrong, what is ugly, what is putrid.
At first, when I listen, I hear nothing but distracted webs of words—
Trying to pull me from my important thoughts, worries, and fears.
At first, when I stop, I fuss—

I itch and I yawn, I sit down and get back up, I eat and
I drink.
Over time, I remain exhausted.
Over time, I remain thin.
Used.
Depleted.
I am too young, yet a part of me has died.
Something small, in the depths of my being,
In the crook of my heart,
Within the core of my soul says,
Wait!

I am beautiful.
I am magnificent.
I am a wonder.
Show me.
Set me free.
Let me loose to the winds;
I will leave laughter on the breeze—
Bringing joy to this world,
And to the next.
There is laughter as fresh as the morning dew resting on the
reds of my lips.
This time, when I rest, I coo, with motherly love to
a child—
You are kind, you are loved, you are worthy.
When I stop to see, I find wondrous things—
I see what is good, what is right, what is whole, what
is life-giving.
Then I stop to listen and I am quiet.
I catch the last few notes of the chickadees' proclamation

Chick-a-dee-dee-dee!
Finally, when I stop, I remain still—
My eyelids gently close and then open; silence and stillness wrap me like a lover's touch; I am satiated.

Go to the Day

Go to the day—
Go find the day worth living.
Overturn stones—
This is where the sun's rays reside.

Go to the mountain—
And if not the mountain,
To the sea;
And if not to the sea,
To the lake;
And if not to the lake,
To the meadow;
And if not to the meadow,
To the forests;
And if not to the forests,
To the grass;
And if not to the grass,
To the dirt;
And if not to the dirt,
To the breeze;
And if not to the breeze—

If you are locked away,
If you are kept from the freedoms of our home,
Then go to where you once were;
And if you cannot—
Know,
You will return to your home.

A Moment's Musings

Goodbye?
What really is goodbye?
I have never been one for goodbyes.
I miss you?
Sure, I have missed comfort, knowing, and familiarity—
But the stranger's sofa!
The unknown!
The new!
It grows old.
"You will be lonely."
I love being with me—
Me is so wondrous, fascinating, intriguing, even funny.
Crowds are where I am left awash—
Too many words,
Too many voices,
Too many crowded thoughts and ideas.
Yippee! I will be left on my own.
What a treasure not many of us are left to experience.
I am not abandoned;
I could reach out any time.
That dastardly technology allows for people to
poke around—
Question my certainty,
Question my path,
Question my knowing.
I snarl from my den at those who dare cross me.
I have been trained to be meek,
To *trust and obey* . . .

Yes, in myself.
I was strong once, you know.
. . . I will be again.
Just you wait.
I will be like a phoenix rising from the ashes.
Born again.
Wild and free.
People will look in awe but I will be in the clouds where their words cannot reach.
I will only heed the hum of the heavens and the whispers of a starry night's sky.
I will rest on my perch in the forests where lightning bugs paint portraits of love.
My darling will wait for me down below.
Their arms open for me to come and, most importantly, to go,
Our passionate loving will carry me through.
I am never alone.
Our spirits soar,
As lovers do.

She Is Hope

Aaaah!
Blinking eyes lower to meet her—
She is wee in size,
Delicate in colour,
Slight in form.
Life—
What a brilliant,
Breathtaking sight.
"I can't believe they are growing."
Tiny seedlings populate rich potting soil;
They are hope.
She is life;
She is hope.

How I am feeling; I am just a wee seedling
Requiring so much tender
Love and care.
Precarious in nature,
At the mercy of the balance,
At the mercy of dedication—
Dedication to love:
Nourish,
Hydrate,
Replenish.

For the First Time in a Long Time

The virus came
          And the people took to the streets
Families played
For the first time in a long time
We stopped the cars with our assertive hands
          And daring glares
We stood alone on the bridge
For the first time in a long time
We said hello to a friend
Asked for help
Lent a hand
For the first time in a long time
We are scared
We are uncertain
We are lost
For the first time in a long time
We are at peace
We can rest
There is room for change
For the first time in a long time
I hope that nothing stays the same
I have rested and read good books
I am hopeful
For the first time in a long time

I am a white Canadian woman, I have written these words on indigenous Treaty 1 Territory from a place of privilege and desire for systemic change.

They Are Four

"She suffers at her own hand,"
Coo the crones.
"Bless her,"
They pray in unison—
Their cackles light up the night.
She wonders what there could possibly be to laugh at.
A thick brew alleviates much of the day, and the
crones dance.
They are four—
The wicked,
The kind,
The ugly,
The pearl.
Their crooked fingers lock as they encircle a blazing fire.
"Wheee,"
They canter merrily 'round.
Her heart is dense, and the light of the crones
confounds her.
The four crammed into a wee shack at the bottom of
the alley—

Plagued by restless weather and the scrutiny of the neighbouring town.
They laugh as if they own a secret.
They dance as if they do not care.
They gather as if they love one another.
They live as if the steel bars aren't there.
"Witches," some sneer.
"Devil maidens."
"Strange things."
"Never married."
"Poor dears, lost their way."
She has a secret of her own—
Slipping out each night to observe their ritual.
Oh, and bless her, they know.
"I want to be like you," she sighs.
Eyes glazed by the light of the moon,
She peers through thick grape vines,
Hops, and ivy.